Current Hits for Teens

7 Graded Selections for Intermediate Pianists

Arranged by
Dan Coates

Teenage students love being able to play popular pieces by their favorite recording artists or from blockbuster movies and TV shows. This collection includes accessible arrangements of pop and movie hits from Doctor Who, fun., Bruno Mars and many more! The arrangements are "teacher friendly," while remaining faithful to the sound of the original recording. In this intermediate collection, 16th-note rhythms are introduced, as well as octaves and increased left-hand arpeggiation.

Produced by
Alfred Music
P.O. Box 10003
Van Nuys, CA 91410-0003
alfred.com

Printed in USA.

ISBN-10: 0-7390-9609-5
ISBN-13: 978-0-7390-9609-3

Cover Images
A piano keyboard waves on white: © shutterstock.com / Dr. Cloud •
stage with light and smoke background: © shutterstock.com / Filipe B. Varela

DOCTOR WHO THEME

By RON GRAINER
Arranged by Dan Coates

FALLING SLOWLY

Words and Music by
GLEN HANSARD and MARKETA IRGLOVA
Arranged by Dan Coates

Slowly, with expression

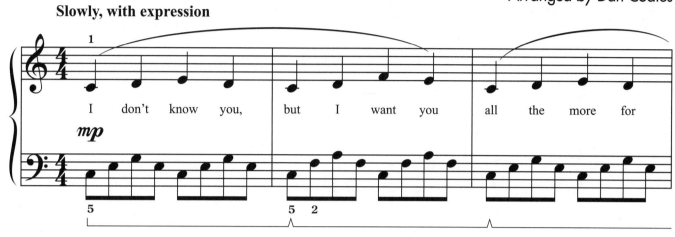

I don't know you, but I want you all the more for

that. Words fall through me and al - ways fool me

and I can't re - act. Games that nev - er a -

mount to more than they're | meant will play them - selves | out.

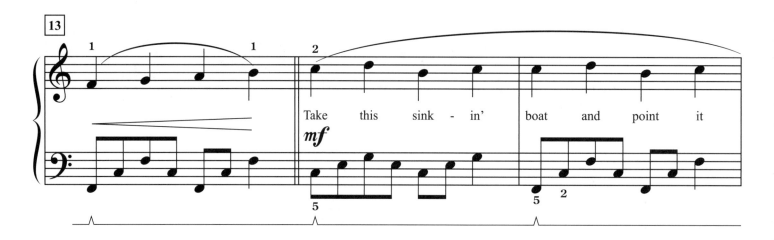

Take this sink - in' boat and point it

mf

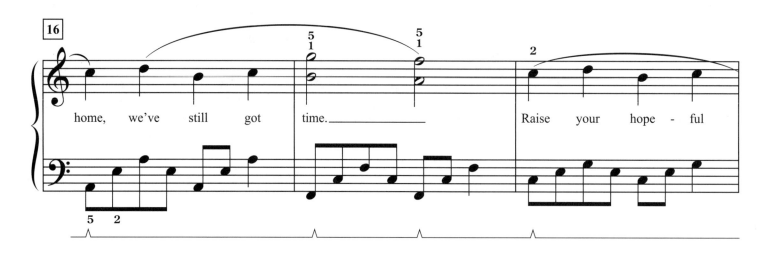

home, we've still got time._____ | Raise your hope - ful

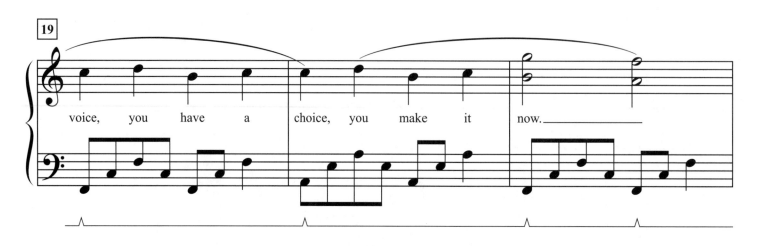

voice, you have a | choice, you make it | now._____

Fall - in' slow - ly, sing your mel - o - dy, I'll sing it loud.

HOME

Words and Music by
DREW PEARSON and GREG HOLDEN
Arranged by Dan Coates

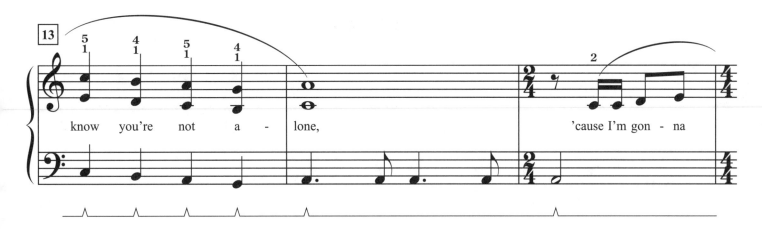

know you're not a - lone, 'cause I'm gon - na

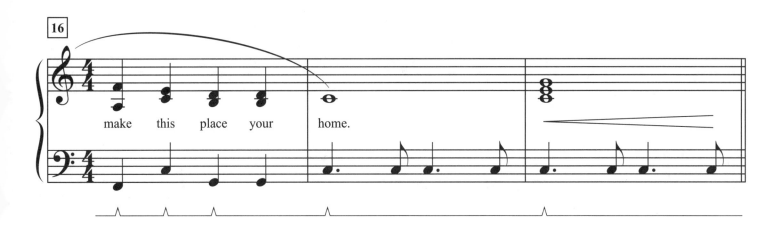

make this place your home.

2., 3. Set - tle down, it - 'll all be clear.

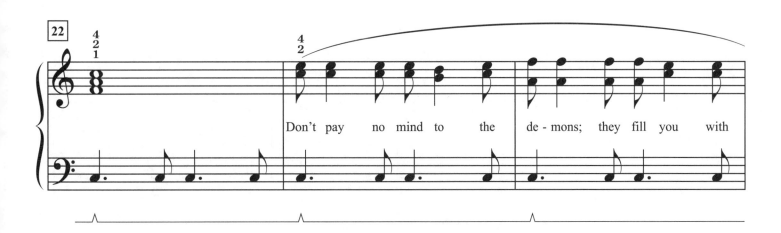

Don't pay no mind to the de - mons; they fill you with

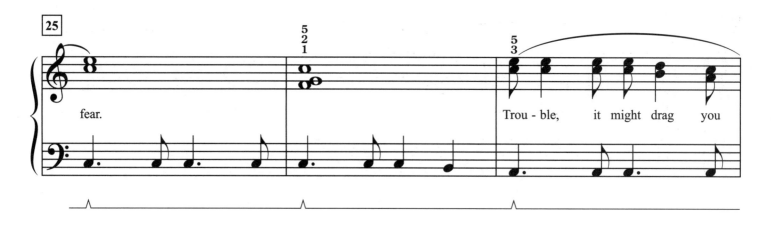

fear. Trou - ble, it might drag you

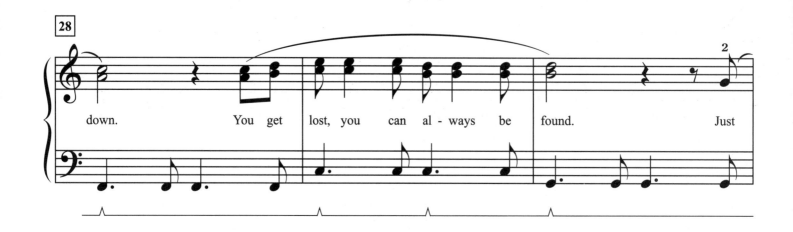

down. You get lost, you can al - ways be found. Just

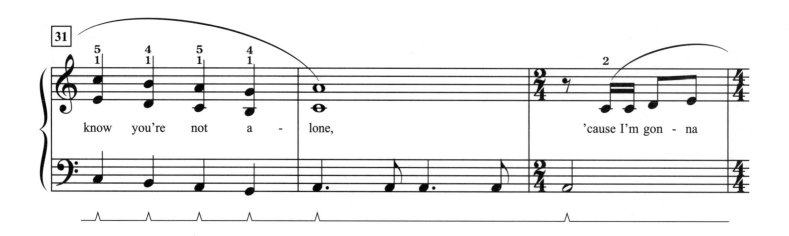

know you're not a - lone, 'cause I'm gon - na

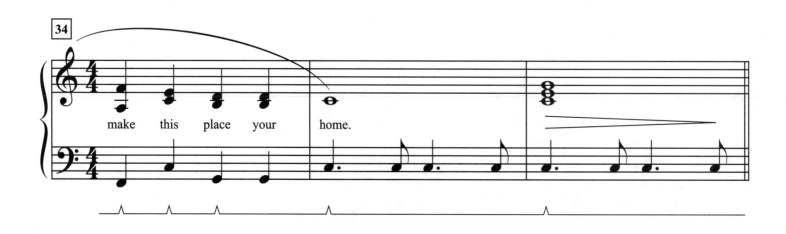

make this place your home.

JUST GIVE ME A REASON

Words and Music by NATE RUESS,
ALECIA MOORE and JEFF BHASKER
Arranged by Dan Coates

Lyrics:

Right from the start you were a thief, you stole my heart and I your will-ing vic-tim. I let you see the parts of me that weren't all that pret-ty, and with ev-'ry touch you fixed them. Now

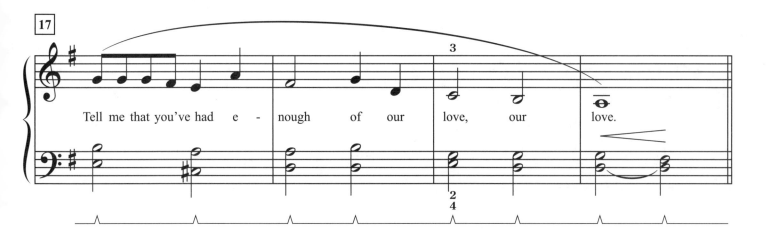

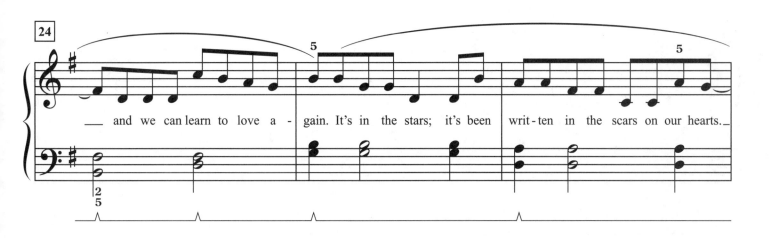

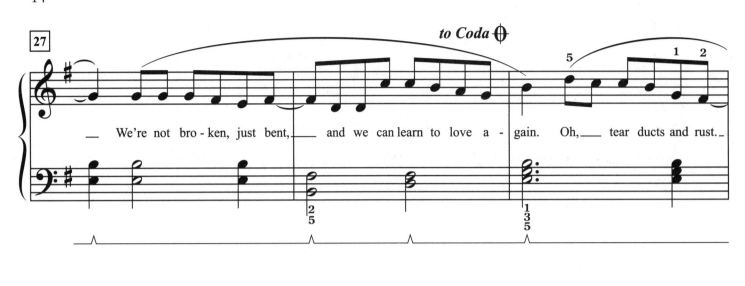

to Coda ⊕

We're not bro-ken, just bent,___ and we can learn to love a-gain. Oh,___ tear ducts and rust.___

___ I'll___ fix it for us.___ We're col-lect-ing dust.___ But our love's___ e-nough.___

___ You're___ hold-ing it in.___ You're pour-ing a drink.___ No___ noth-ing is as

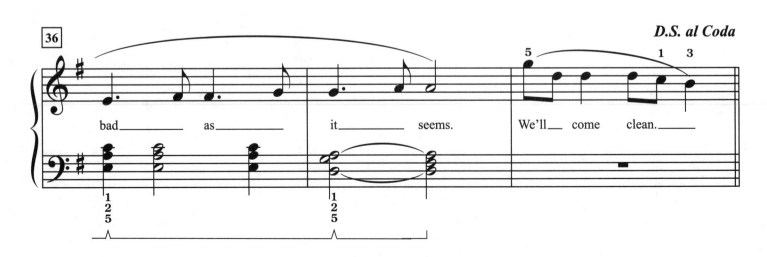

D.S. al Coda

bad___ as___ it___ seems. We'll___ come clean.___

Coda

gain. Oh,_____ we can learn to love a - gain. Oh,_____

_____ we can learn to love a - gain.

We're not bro - ken, just bent,_____ and we can learn to love a - gain.

mp

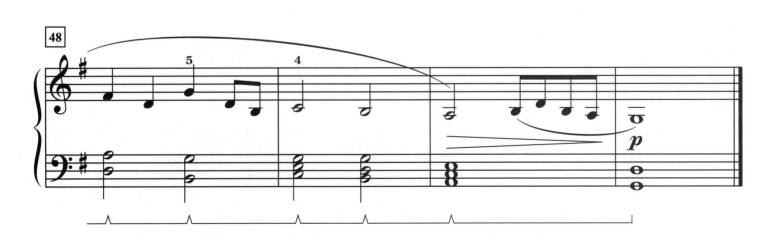

p

SOME NIGHTS

Words and Music by NATE RUESS,
JEFF BHASKER, ANDREW DOST and JACK ANTONOFF
Arranged by Dan Coates

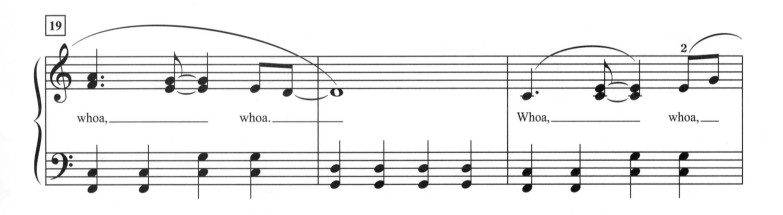

some nights, I wish___ that this all___ would end,___ 'cause I could use some friends for a

change. And some nights, I'm scared___ you'll for - get me a - gain, some

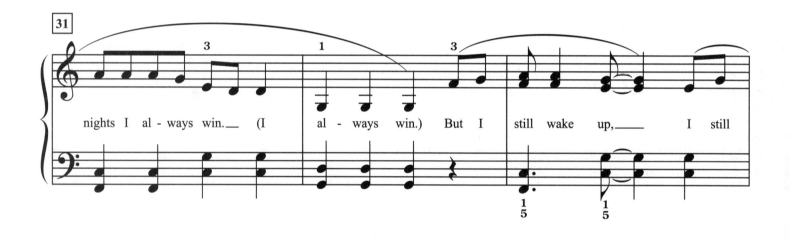

nights I al - ways win.___ (I al - ways win.) But I still wake up,___ I still

see your ghost.___ Oh, Lord, I'm still not sure___ what I stand for, oh, whoa.___

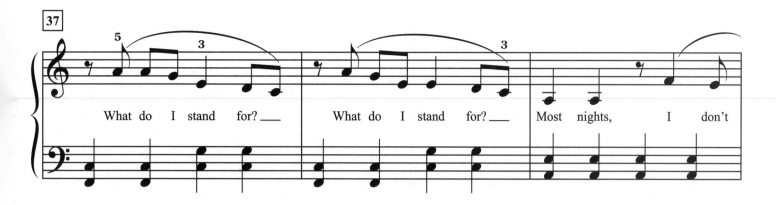

What do I stand for? ___ What do I stand for? ___ Most nights, I don't

know ___ an - y - more. ___ Whoa, ___ whoa, whoa, ___ whoa, ___

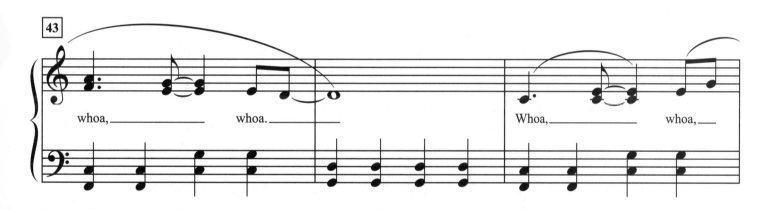

whoa, ___ whoa. Whoa, ___ whoa, ___

whoa, ___ whoa, ___ whoa, ___ whoa. ___

WHEN I WAS YOUR MAN

Words and Music by PHILIP LAWRENCE,
ANDREW WYATT, BRUNO MARS and ARI LEVINE
Arranged by Dan Coates

WIDE AWAKE

Words and Music by KATY PERRY, BONNIE McKEE,
LUKASZ GOTTWALD, MAX MARTIN and HENRY WALTER
Arranged by Dan Coates

Moderately bright

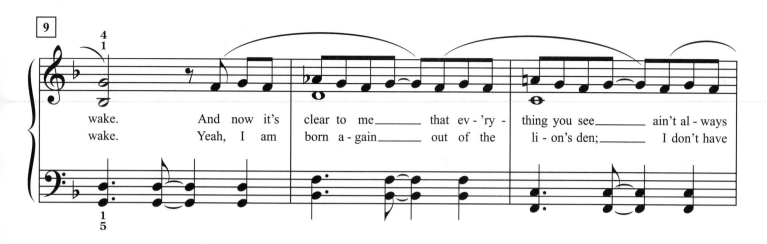

wake. And now it's | clear to me_____ that ev-'ry- | thing you see_____ ain't al-ways
wake. Yeah, I am | born a-gain_____ out of the | li-on's den;_____ I don't have

what it seems._ I'm wide a - | wake. Yeah, I was | dream-ing for_____ so long.
to pre-tend._ And it's too | late. The sto-ry's | o-ver now;_____ the end.

I wish I knew | then what I know

now; would-n't dive | in, would-n't bow | down. Grav-i-ty

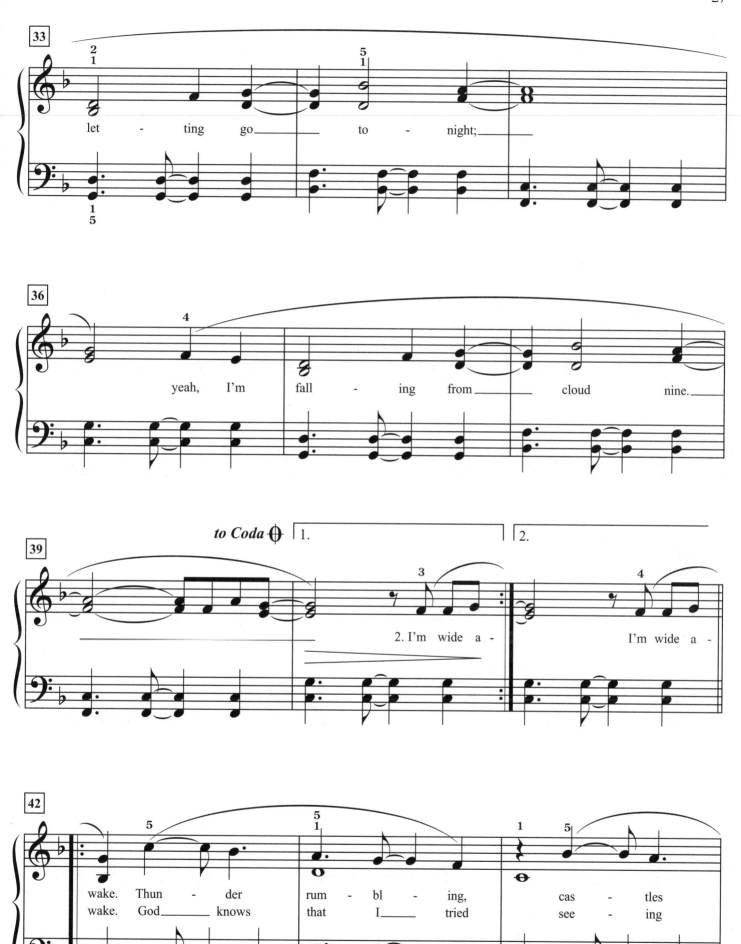

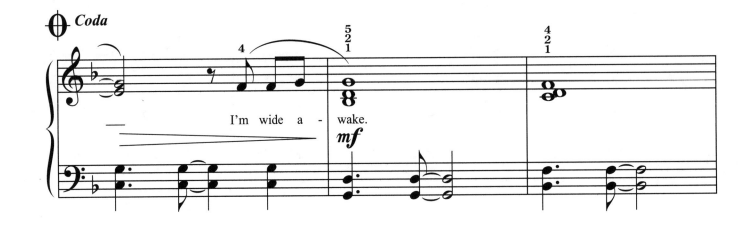